Short and Tall

by Rod Theodorou and Carole Telford

Contents

RIGBY
INTERACTIVE
LIBRARY

Illustrations by Sheila Townsend and Trevor Dunton
Color reproduction by Track QSP
Printed in China

00 99 98 97 96
10 9 8 7 6 5 4 3 2 1

ISBN 1-57572-065-5

Library of Congress Cataloging-in-Publication Data
Theodorou, Rod.
   Short and tall / by Rod Theodorou and Carole Telford;
[illustrations by Sheila Townsend and Trevor Dunton].
      p. cm. — (Animal opposites)
  Includes index.
  Summary: Compares the physical characteristics, habitat, feeding patterns, and behavior of the shrew and giraffe, as determined by their size.
  ISBN 1-57572-065-5 (lib. bdg.)
  1. Animals—Juvenile literature. 2. Shrews—Juvenile literature.
3. Giraffe—Juvenile literature. 4. Body size—Juvenile literature.
[1. Shrews. 2. Giraffe. 3. Body size.] I. Telford, Carole, 1961–
II. Townsend, Sheila, ill. III. Dunton, Trevor, ill. IV. Title.
V. Series: Theodorou, Rod. Animal opposites.
QL49.T349 1996
591.5—dc20   95-42019
                                                             CIP
                                                               AC

Photographic Acknowledgments
Attilio Calegari/OSF(Oxford Scientific Films) pp4, 6 *bl*; Norbert Rosing/OSF pp5, 7; Presstige Pictures/OSF p6 *t*; Barrie Watts/OSF pp6 *br*, 10; Philip Sharpe/OSF pp8, 13; Mark Deeble and Victoria Stone/OSF p9; M. Wendler Okapia/OSF p11; Mark Hamblin/OSF p14; Rafi Ben-Shahar/OSF pp15, 19, 21; Tim Shepherd/OSF p20; Terry Button/OSF p16; Richard Packwood/OSF p17; Stouffer Enterprises Inc. Animals Animals/OSF p18
Front cover: Attilio Calegari/OSF; Richard Packwood/OSF; Trevor Clifford

lizard

shrew

toad

Some animals are short.
Some animals are tall.

giraffe

ostrich

camel

This animal is a shrew.
A shrew is so tiny and short, it could sit in the palm of your hand.

This animal is
a giraffe.
A giraffe is large
and tall.
It can grow as
high as a
double-decker
bus.

There are shrews all over
the world.
Some live in warm countries.
Some live in cold countries.

water shrew

common shrew

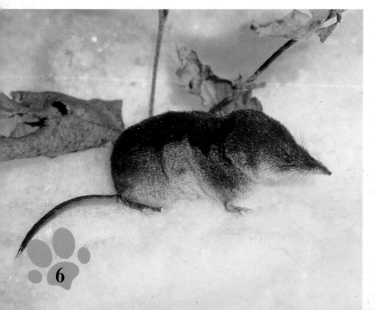

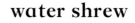
pygmy shrew

Giraffes live in Africa.
They live in groups called herds.

Shrews live among leaves and grass.
They can dart into small spaces.

Giraffes
live out in
the open.
Their spots
can help
them hide
from their
enemies.

Shrews can see and smell very well.
They can watch out for their enemies.

Giraffes are so tall, they can see a long way off. Giraffes watch out for lions.

Shrews can hide from their enemies in small holes.

Giraffes can run fast.
They can kick their enemies.

Many bigger animals hunt shrews.
This owl has killed a shrew.

Only big, fierce animals like
lions can kill a giraffe.

Shrews eat insects and other small animals.
This shrew is eating a worm.

Giraffes
eat leaves.
They can
eat leaves that
other animals
cannot reach.

A mother shrew has lots of babies.
They need to grow fur to keep warm.

A mother
giraffe has
one baby
a year.
When it is
born, it has
a long way
to drop.

Baby shrews are safe in their nest. When they grow bigger, they have to leave the nest.

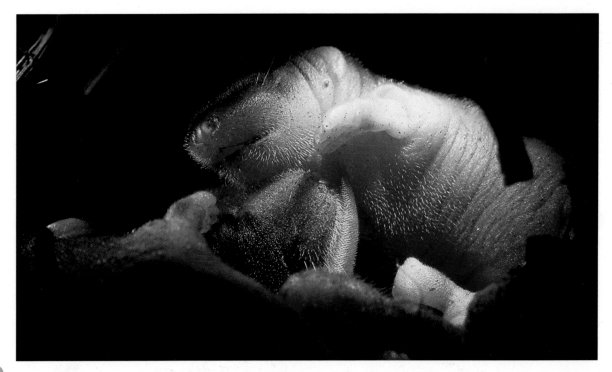

A baby giraffe has nowhere safe to hide.
It must quickly learn to run.

AMAZING FACTS!

When a mother shrew
leaves the nest for food,
her babies follow her.
They hold onto each other's tails!

A baby giraffe can run with its mother only 10 hours after it is born!

A giraffe has to spread its legs apart to drink water.

Index